A FIRST LOOK BOOK

Fossils

Neil Curtis

Franklin Watts

London   New York   Toronto   Sydney

©1984 Franklin Watts Ltd

First published in Great Britain
   1984 by
Franklin Watts Ltd
12a Golden Square
London W1

First published in the USA by
Franklin Watts Inc.
387 Park Avenue South
New York
N.Y. 10016

UK ISBN: 0 863 13 129 8
US ISBN: 0-531-03773-8
Library of Congress Catalog Card
   Number: 83-51439

Designed by
Jim Marks

Edited by
Judith Maxwell

Illustrated by
Mike Atkinson, Jim Marks, Ralph
   Stobbart, Steve Wilson

Photographs supplied by
Heather Angel, British Museum
   (Natural History), RIDA, Shell

Technical consultant
Dr Richard Moody

Printed in Great Britain by
   Cambus Litho, East Kilbride

A FIRST LOOK BOOK

Fossils

Contents

What are fossils?

▽This cockroach, preserved in amber, is millions of years old. When a tree such as a fir or pine is damaged, sap bleeds from the wound. As it trickles out it may trap an insect. The sap slowly turns into amber, hardening around the insect's body.

Fossils are the remains of plants or animals that lived many years ago. When they died, their remains lay under mud or sand. Over millions of years these changed into rock. Some fossils are also preserved in ice, or tar. Insects and spiders can be found in the hardened tree sap, which is called amber.

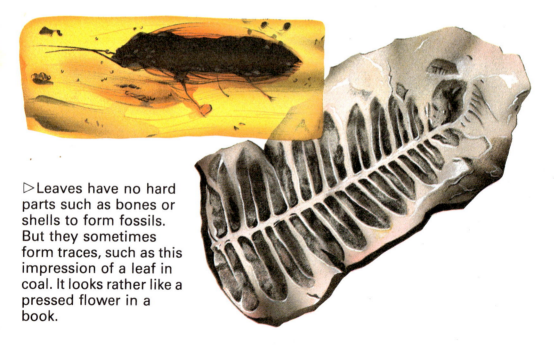

▷Leaves have no hard parts such as bones or shells to form fossils. But they sometimes form traces, such as this impression of a leaf in coal. It looks rather like a pressed flower in a book.

4

Fossils tell us much about life on Earth over millions of years. Some fossils are 3,500 million years old. Others have been preserved for only a few thousand years.

Most fossils are formed from the hard parts of animals, such as a skeleton or shell. But sometimes the traces of a soft-bodied worm or an animal's footprint may be found. The delicate outlines of a leaf may be preserved in coal, which is formed from the remains of dead trees.

△A fossil of the first bird, *Archaeopteryx*, shows a creature very different from birds today. It was similar to a reptile with teeth and clawed fingers. But the traces of its feathers can be clearly seen.

How are fossils formed?

When an animal dies, its flesh soon rots away or is eaten by other animals. Bones last much longer. Fish bones, for example, sink to the bottom of the ocean, lake or river in which the fish lived. Most skeletons break up in the water, but some lie undisturbed in the gravel or sand. They settle and are gradually buried under layers of more mud and sand.

◁ **1** This ammonite lived in the sea 150 million years ago.
2 When it died, its shell became buried under mud on the seabed.
3 The mud hardened into rock around the shell, forming a fossil.

▽ **4** The fossil may dissolve away, leaving a hole. If the hole is not filled, an empty *mould* of the shell is left.
5 If the hole fills with mud or sand, a cast of the fossil forms, looking like the ammonite shell.

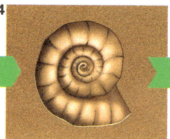

Over many years, the sand and mud harden into rock, locking the skeleton inside. In time, the river or lake may dry up, or the line of the seashore may change. Rocks which were once under water may become dry land. As the surface of these rocks is eroded, worn away by wind and rain, fossils deep in the rock are revealed.

Land animals and plants can be preserved in a similar way too, but most fossils are of water-dwelling creatures.

△ These human footprints were made over 3 million years ago in East Africa. The earth later hardened into rock, preserving the prints as fossils.

How we use fossils

△Huge, swampy forests covered the Earth over 280 million years ago. Insects and reptiles lived in them. Giant ferns grew there and rush-like horsetails. Some trees had scaly trunks.

We use "fossils" every day in our homes and at work. Coal, oil and natural gas are all fossil fuels which we burn to make heat and electricity. Our cars run on oil and petrol. All these fossil fuels come from the remains of ancient plants and animals. Today, we depend on them to run our industries, transport and communications.

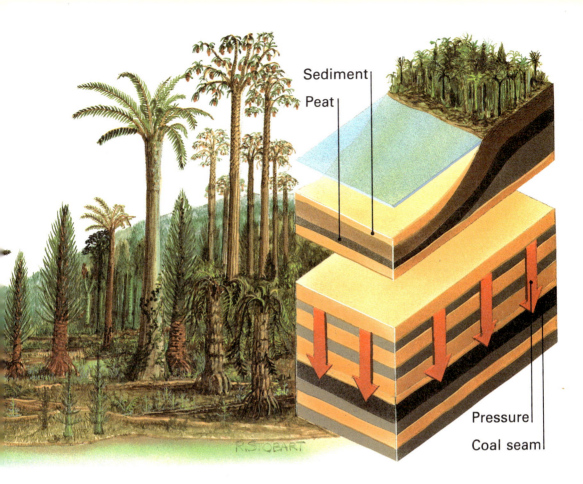

Sediment

Peat

Pressure

Coal seam

R.STOBART

Coal is a shiny black rock formed from the remains of huge trees which grew millions of years ago. Oil is also millions of years old. It was formed from the bodies of countless tiny sea creatures. Natural gas may have come from oil heated up inside the Earth. Or it may have formed from plants which rotted in swamps.

△Dead plants fell into the forest swamps. The water stopped them from rotting away. Instead, the plants formed thick layers of peat. Forests near the sea were sometimes flooded. The sea water left behind sand and mud which later hardened to rock. The peat was pressed beneath forming coal.

What fossils can tell us

Fossils tell us much about the history of the Earth. Many plants and animals which lived millions of years ago are now extinct. Others looked very different from their modern descendants. But some plants and animals look very much the same today as they did in ages long past.

▽ Scientists can trace how the elephant has changed, or evolved, by studying fossils of its bones. *Moeritherium*, an ancestor of the elephant, was the size of a pig. Later, elephants became bigger, with trunks and tusks. These helped them to fight off their enemies.

Scientists can tell the age of rocks from the fossils they contain. They can also tell what the climate was like when a fossil plant or animal was alive. The fossil of a palm tree found in rocks of northern Scotland shows that the weather must have been much warmer when the plant was growing there. Fossils may also give scientists new ideas. Remains of the same kind of land animals have been found in places as far apart as Africa and South America. This makes scientists think that the continents were once joined together.

△ The peppered moth shows how animals can change to fit into new surroundings. The pale moth once matched the tree bark on which it rested. This helped it to hide from its enemies. Then factories were built and their smoke blackened the trees. Soon a darker form of peppered moth became common.

11

Fossils come to life

Small animals can be found as complete fossils. But often only a few bones of larger animals are found. Scientists can use these to build up a picture of the whole animal.

Scientists compare the fossils they find with the remains of animals that are alive today. They might discover fossil teeth in rocks that were once under the sea. Looking at the sea creatures of today, they may find, for example, that the fossils look very similar to shark's teeth. If so, the rest of the animal may have looked like a shark too. If other fossils from the same animal can be found, scientists are able to build up an accurate picture of the unknown creature.

◁*Parasaurolophus* lived millions of years ago. From fossils of its skull we know that it had a hollow crest on its head. Scientists have studied living animals with crests to discover what they were used for. The crest may have helped the animal to breathe under water, or to improve its sense of smell. Or it could have been used as a sort of flag to signal to other dinosaurs.

13

Sea creatures in dry stone

◁Volcanoes spew out hot ash and lava which cools into rock. In time, the rock wears away to tiny grains of sand or mud. Rivers carry these grains to the sea.

◁Sand and mud grains (sediment) carried to the sea 500 million years ago may have buried the remains of a sea creature called a trilobite. More layers of sediment built up and then slowly hardened into a new form of rock.

Fossils of creatures that once lived in the sea are sometimes found on a mountainside. This happens because the Earth's surface is made up of giant plates which move so slowly that nobody notices. When the edges of the plates push against each other, the surface is forced upwards. Rocks that were once under the sea are pushed up slowly, over millions of years, to form mountains on dry land.

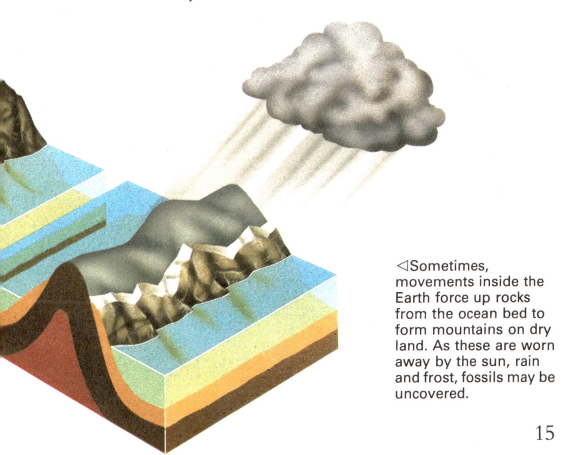

◁Sometimes, movements inside the Earth force up rocks from the ocean bed to form mountains on dry land. As these are worn away by the sun, rain and frost, fossils may be uncovered.

15

Where to find fossils

▽ Ammonites are among the fossils most often found. Cliffs by the sea are good places to look for fossils. As the cliffs are worn away by waves crashing against them, fossils in the rocks may be revealed. Some may be washed from the cliffs on to the seashore.

Most fossils were formed under water and are best preserved there. So it is best to start hunting for fossils in rocks that were once under water. Sandstone, clay, shale and limestone are good rocks to choose. A special kind of guide, called a geological map, will show you the places where these rocks can be found

Fossils up to 3,500 million years old have been found, but you are more likely to find them in rocks formed less than 600 million years ago. The geological map will show where rocks of the right age and type can be found. Most rocks are buried under soil, so look for places where the soil has been removed. Cliffs, quarries and river banks are good places for fossil hunting, as are the cuttings dug for railways and new roads. You may need permission before starting to dig.

△Fossils can also be found in clay pits. Recently, a fossil hunter made an exciting discovery in a clay pit in Surrey, England. It was the remains of a new dinosaur, which has been nicknamed "Claws". In this picture, museum workers are carefully removing the fossil skeleton. The study of fossils is called palaeontology.

Collecting fossils

You may be lucky and spot a fossil lying on a beach, but most collectors need to prepare more carefully for an expedition. First choose a likely site, using a geological map. You should wear warm clothes and strong boots for rough ground. Rocks, cliffs, and quarries are all places in which to take care. Always wear a helmet where falling rocks are a danger.

Some equipment is useful. A geological hammer will help to break up rocks, as will a hard tool called a cold chisel. Use all tools with care, to avoid damaging your fossil. Keep a magnifying glass to look at discoveries.

You can protect your fossils by wrapping them carefully in newspaper, but boxes give better protection. Label each find with the place and date of discovery. Fossils in museums have been specially treated by experts to protect them from damage.

△These tools are useful for collecting fossils.
▷Experts in museums can build up whole skeletons from pieces of bones. This is a skeleton of the dinosaur called *Iguanodon*.

18

The fossil record

Rocks are found in layers, one on top of the other. The oldest rocks are at the bottom and the youngest at the top. Scientists can work out the age of a rock by means of radiometric dating. All rocks are radioactive, but the radio-activity is slowly lost over many years. By measuring how much is left, scientists know how old a rock is. They can also tell the age of its fossils.

In this way, scientists see how living things have changed over millions of years. They can make a record of life on Earth, as shown on the chart.

▷Scientists divide the Earth's history into eras and periods. The Precambrian extends from the birth of the Earth up to 570 million years ago. After this come the Palaeozoic, Mesozoic and Cenozoic eras. Each era is divided into periods.

Millions of years ago	Period
2–Present	Quaternary
65–2	Tertiary
136–65	Cretaceous
190–136	Jurassic
225–190	Triassic
280–225	Permian
345–280	Carboniferous
395–345	Devonian
430–395	Silurian
500–430	Ordovician
570–500	Cambrian
4,500–570	Precambrian

Key	Cenozoic era
	Mesozoic era
	Palaeozoic era
	Precambrian era

Meaning	Animals and plants
The fourth formation	The age of humans.
The third formation	Many mammals, birds and flowering plants emerge, as well as new animals without backbones.
Chalky	The flowering plants appear while many groups of animals, including the dinosaurs, become extinct.
After the Jura mountains	Ginkgoes and cycads dominate the plant life. Dinosaurs rule the land and the first bird appears.
The rocks can be divided into three groups	The first dinosaurs and mammals appear.
After a town in Russia	New reptiles and plants appear on land. Many ammonites swim in the seas.
Coal bearing	The first land animals — reptiles — appear. Much of the land is covered in swampy forests.
After the county of Devon	Plants cover the land and the first forests grow. Animals, called amphibians, appear which live part of their life on land.
After an ancient Welsh tribe	The first land plants appear. The seas contain many different fishes and huge sea scorpions.
After another Welsh tribe	Sea-living plants and animals, including brachiopods, trilobites, graptolites and the first fishes.
After the Latin name of Wales	Sea-living plants and animals, such as jellyfish, sponges, corals and trilobites.
Before the Cambrian	First simple creatures appeared 3,500 million years ago.

The beginning of life

△ The planet Earth probably formed about 4,500 million years ago, from a cloud of gas and dust. As the planet heated up, a crust formed around it. This crust was the Earth's surface. Volcanoes threw out lava into an atmosphere thick with gases. Through clouds of ammonia, carbon dioxide and steam, lightning flashed and heavy rains fell.

The first fossils of living things are found in rocks about 3,500 million years old. The Earth itself is much older. In its early state, the planet Earth was so hot that water boiled to steam. It swirled with other gases about the surface. But there was no oxygen, the gas which animals need to live. Later, the Earth cooled. Lightning flashed and rain fell, forming pools of water. Life began in these pools.

A mixture of gases, sunlight and lightning flashes may have made the chemicals from which life formed. In time, cells developed and millions of years later came the first plants. Plants use sunlight, water and carbon dioxide gas to make food, giving off oxygen as they do so. As oxygen built up in the atmosphere, the first animals appeared. These soft-bodied creatures had no hard parts to leave as fossils.

The time of ancient life

Few traces are left of the Earth's early plants and animals. But in rocks 570 million years old, remains of animals with hard skins or shells appear. This was the beginning of the Palaeozoic era, the "time of ancient life".

Many plants and animals lived in the seas. Most of the animals had no backbones and many have since died out. Among these were trilobites, graptolites and sea scorpions 3 m (10 ft) long. But sea lilies, sea snails and brachiopods still live in the ocean today.

The Palaeozoic era is divided into periods. In the Ordovician period, 500–430 million years ago, fishes appeared. These were the first animals with backbones. At this time the land was bare, but then tiny plants started to grow. By the Carboniferous period, 345–280 million years ago, there were huge forests. Animals, including reptiles, were living on land.

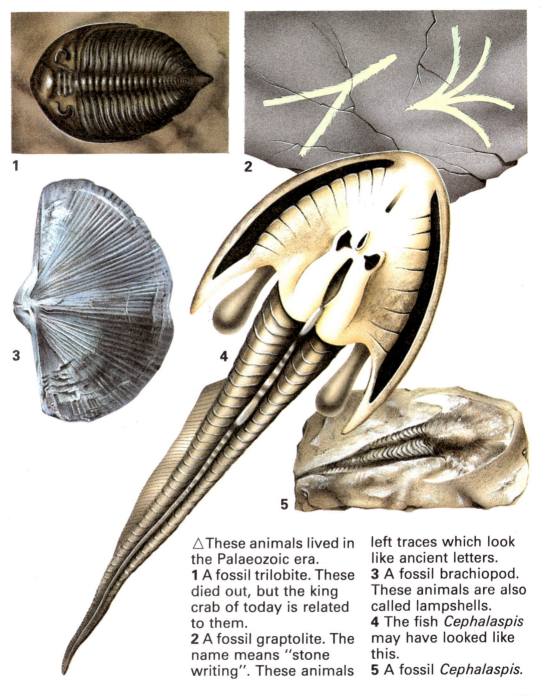

△These animals lived in the Palaeozoic era.
1 A fossil trilobite. These died out, but the king crab of today is related to them.
2 A fossil graptolite. The name means "stone writing". These animals left traces which look like ancient letters.
3 A fossil brachiopod. These animals are also called lampshells.
4 The fish *Cephalaspis* may have looked like this.
5 A fossil *Cephalaspis.*

25

The time of middle life

△ The Mesozoic era —
the "time of middle life"
— began 225 million
years ago.

▽ Here are some
Mesozoic fossils.
1 Ammonites were
common in Mesozoic
seas. They are related to
the octopus and squid.
2 Sea urchins, found in
Mesozoic rocks, live in
today's oceans too.
3 Dinosaur eggs.
Dinosaurs were reptiles,
and so laid eggs.

The Mesozoic era began 225 million years ago. Among common fossils found in its rocks are those of ammonites and belemnites — animals related to the octopus and squid. By the end of this era, birds and mammals had appeared and flowering plants were spreading over the land. But the Mesozoic is truly the Age of Reptiles. Great dinosaurs roamed on land, from the enormous 100-tonne *Supersaurus* to creatures no bigger than a blackbird. Reptiles such as ichthyosaurs and plesiosaurs lived in water. Others, including *Pteranodon*, took to the air.

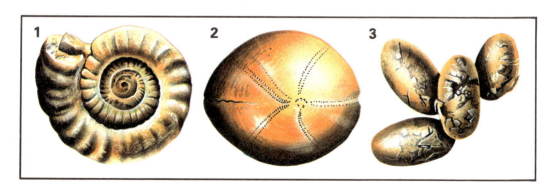

△Reptiles, called
ichthyosaurs (above)
and plesiosaurs (below),
lived in Mesozoic seas.
They probably swam
rather as seals do today.
Some people think that
the famous "Loch Ness
monster" may be a
plesiosaur.

△A fossil ichthyosaur.

The time of recent life

△ The Cenozoic era — the "time of recent life" — began 65 million years ago. We are living in this era today.

By the start of the Cenozoic era, 65 million years ago, many of the Mesozoic animals had died out. The groups which disappeared included the dinosaurs, ichthyosaurs, plesiosaurs and ammonites. Nobody knows why they vanished from the Earth so suddenly. In the Mesozoic era, mammals were small, timid creatures, which hid from the meat-eating dinosaurs. Mammals have hair and give birth to live young. When the dinosaurs died out many new mammals took their place. Fossils show that during the Cenozoic ere there were many new plants and birds as well, such as the meat-eating *Diatryma*, which was 2m (7 ft) tall.

Slowly, the strange new mammals gave way to the familiar ones we know today — dogs, cats, horses and elephants. The first human fossils have been found in rocks about 5 million years old.

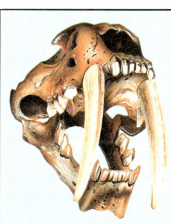

◁The fossil skull of a sabre-toothed cat shows its enormous front teeth. These big cats lived 40–20 million years ago. They were about 2 m (7 ft) long.

△The world's climate has changed often in our era. At times there have been Ice Ages, when large parts of the Earth have been covered by glaciers. Woolly mammoths lived during the last Ice Age, and they have been found preserved in ice in Siberia, USSR.

Glossary

Here is a list of some of the technical words used in this book.

Clay
A soft, earthy rock which is easy to mould when wet but hard and brittle when dry. It may be found beneath some types of soil.

Cold chisel
A chisel is a sharp-edged tool used for cutting. A cold chisel is a strong chisel used for cutting metal or rock.

Erosion
The action of wind, water, rain and other forces, that breaks up rocks.

Geology
The science in which the Earth is studied.

Glacier
A great mass of ice which forms as piles of snow grow deeper and harden. Glaciers often form in the valleys between mountains in cold countries.

Horsetail
A primitive plant with hollow, jointed stems.

◁Oil is a fossil fuel. It collects in "pockets" in the rocks. Wells are drilled down to these pockets from rigs, such as that shown here.

Fossil facts

Limestone
A rock formed, usually in the sea, from the chalky shells of sea creatures which have broken up and fallen to the seabed.

Palaeontology
The study of fossils.

Radioactive
Substances which give off rays or particles are called radioactive.

Sandstone
A rock which is formed from sand, usually in the sea or in deserts.

Scale tree
An ancient tree related to modern club mosses.

Sediment
Any solid material present in water. It sinks and settles on the bottom.

Shale
A rock formed from mud. It has a layered appearance.

Here are some interesting facts about fossils and prehistoric life.

About 65 million years ago, many different groups of land and sea-living animals and plants vanished. Even the mighty dinosaurs disappeared. They seemed to die out very suddenly at the end of the Mesozoic era. There are at least forty different ideas to explain why this happened.

Perhaps the most likely suggestion is that the climate changed quite suddenly and these creatures could not cope with the new conditions.

The tapir is an animal which looks rather like a pig. But it has a nose that resembles a short elephant's trunk. Today, tapirs live in Central and South America and south-east Asia. Scientists find it odd that they should only be found in places so far apart. But fossil finds showed that, millions of years ago, tapirs lived right across Asia, Europe and America.

Their fossils also helped to show that Europe and North America must once have been joined together. For these animals could not have swum across the Atlantic Ocean.

The Carboniferous Period seems to have been a time for giant insects. Dragonflies are quite common today. Their bodies are usually about 5 cm (2 in) long. but the biggest insect ever lived in the carboniferous swamps. It was a dragonfly called *Meganeura*. Its wingspan was 60 cm (2 ft)!

Index